Rebuilding
YOUR TEMPLE
WITH SELF-ESTEEM
—❧—— FROM THE ——❧—
INSIDE OUT

Here is a practical how- to guide to rebuilding and restoring one's self-esteem (value) when it has suffered a decline. This book provides turn-around solutions to the challenges that affect self-esteem, by addressing the: who, what, when, where, why and how self-esteem is central to one's being. Additionally, this work encourages investigation to discover oneself.

Rebuilding YOUR TEMPLE WITH SELF-ESTEEM ❧ FROM THE ❧ INSIDE OUT

DR. JAMES E. BRUCE, SR.

LitPrime
"Your story is our priority"

LitPrime Solutions
21250 Hawthorne Blvd
Suite 500, Torrance, CA 90503
www.litprime.com
Phone: 1-800-981-9893

Published by LitPrime Solutions   11/16/2023

ISBN: 979-8-88703-308-2(sc)
ISBN: 979-8-88703-309-9(hc)
ISBN: 979-8-88703-310-5(e)

Library of Congress Control Number: 2023918919

Contents

Foreword

THIS BOOK CRITICALLY DEALS WITH the topic of self-respect or self-confidence, also known as Self-esteem. Here is a practical how-to guide to rebuilding and restoring ones' self-esteem when it has suffered a decline. This book provides turn-around solutions to the challenges that affect self-esteem, by addressing the: who, what, when, where, why and how self-esteem is central to ones' being.

This book is presented in part by using as a metaphor the rebuilding of a falling down house is a way to highlight the human experience of going from embarrassed to empowered, or from lonely to lively. In a descriptive way, this book demonstrates how to begin and succeed at turning one around from being down and out, to being up and about; from doubt to dominance, or from weeping to winning.

Applying the assessment protocols provided in this guide, the investigator should experience how relatively easy it is to identify the causes for low self-esteem. The reader should be amazed about how simple the process to is towards rebuilding and restoring ones' self-esteem when it has suffered a decline.

Dedication

THIS WORK IS A DEDICATION with congratulations to the many people who can first love their Creator, then feel good about themselves and have love and respect for themselves, and then can feel love and respect for others. Further, this dedication is offered with a prayer and hope for so many people who lack self-love, respect and confidence. The hope is that the benefits of this practical guide to rebuilding your Temple will be understood, accepted and applied. So then maybe more people will become proactive about making progress and moving forward. And as that happens, perhaps the negative words and counter-productive behavior will cease. The eyes will open; the head will rise; the chest will extend; the backbone will again align; and more positive energy will fill our world.

Finally, I would like to thank and pray for all those who have and continue to support me. Also, I encourage the readers to become familiar with the signs of low self-esteem. So that if the low is to be transformed to high, then those who plan to or are ready to take action and turn the situation around, will mark their success.

Introduction

REBUILDING YOUR TEMPLE WITH SELF-ESTEEM-FROM the inside out. As a book title, one might initially be a bit confused as to what is meant by. *Rebuilding your temple with self-esteem- from the inside out.* Perhaps the one word that could raise questions for clarity is the word temple. This practical guide is not dealing with the temple, as in the flat surface alongside the forehead. No, it is not talking about the brick-and-mortar building for the worship of God. The word temple has to do with ones' physical body and their spirit housed within. The other word that is operative is rebuilding. Rebuilding is precisely the goal of this practical guide. The next questions are: what is being rebuilt? And how will the rebuilding be done? The answers are that self-esteem is being rebuilt. And from inside out is the answer for how self-esteem will be rebuilt. The more practical consideration is to know or discover what tools, and methodologies will be used to achieve the state that something of someone has been rebuilt.

This guide includes exercises that will help examine a person's physical, spiritual, social, psychological, financial, present and historical status, which might speak to one's current state of being.

Disclaimer: The author is not a psychologist, psychiatrist, nor a behavioral scientist. However, fortified life experiences with a proven application and results can often add more knowledge than the lessons found in the textbook. This work is presented in simple, easy-to-understand language.

Author's Analysis

W HAT FOLLOWS IN THIS SECTION, is an analysis filled with self-examination questions, thought-provoking topics for discussion, suppositions, objectivities, subjectivities, debatable topics, definitions, and ideas concerning self-esteem- low, high, and normal. This analysis is offered intentionally to stimulate discussion, provide information, and invite the reader to engage with the subject… with a more informed understanding of what self-esteem is.

WHO AM I?

Perhaps one of the greatest personal achievements in life is for one to know oneself. Is that possible? Have you ever pursued this question?

In life, there are so many people who represent themselves, entities, and institutions that seek, and in many instances acquire more factual information about you, more than you can imagine.

In addition to the demographics and analytics they obtain, there is so much more information that can be achieved when the information is combined and analyzed. From the interpreted information about you, many determinations, decisions and final conclusions are drawn. Labels are placed upon you which are intended to suggest or categorize you into a certain group that is designed to be representative of your behavior, character, personality, feelings, and emotions, about your past, present and future. Interestingly, and often, there may be conflict about who or what they say you are. You may find yourself in denial, because you see yourself, otherwise.

WHAT IS YOUR RESPONSE TO THESE QUESTIONS:

WHO AM I?

_____

HAVE YOU EVER THOUGHT, OR ASKED YOURSELF, "WHAT IS MY PURPOSE OR CALLING IN LIFE?"

WHAT DO YOU FEEL OR BELIEVE IS YOUR PURPOSE OR CALLING AT THIS TIME?

_____

Some people serve in certain capacities, with enthusiasm, excitement, and a sense of reward. But at times, the excitement dissipates, and they begin to feel less satisfied, and rarely fulfilled.

CAN YOU IDENTIFY WITH THIS EXPERIENCE? IF SO, HOW?

_____

_____

DR. JAMES E. BRUCE, SR.

WHAT MAKES ME TICK?

Have you ever questioned yourself to get an idea of what drives and motivates you? Why you think, believe, and do what you do? And how you think and feel about yourself and others?

WHAT ARE MY LIKES?

Most people have a sense for what they like. Their likes may even evolve into a favorite, or even something they love. That something could be an object, a person, or an activity. These likes tend to bring about joy, peace, happiness, excitement, inspiration, and motivation, thus impacting one's feelings, emotions, and passions.

EVERYONE HAS SOMETHING THEY LIKE. SHARE SOME THINGS YOU LIKE.

WHAT ARE MY DISLIKES?

Most people have a sense for what they don't like. Their dislikes may even evolve into distastes, or even something they hate. That something could be an object, a person, or an activity. These dislikes tend to impact one's feelings, and emotions, which can bring about stress, anxiety, anger, depression, boredom, or disinterest. These impacted feelings and emotions can lead to one's resistance or complete refusal to be engaged in certain activities.

EVERYONE HAS SOMETHING THEY DON'T LIKE, DOES THIS QUESTION APPLY TO YOU, IF SO, HOW?

WHAT MAKES ME HAPPY?

WHAT ARE THE THINGS, ACTIVITIES, OR PEOPLE THAT MAKE YOU SMILE, LAUGH, FEEL HAPPY, EXCITED, INSPIRED, AND MOTIVATED?

WHAT MAKES ME UNHAPPY?

WHAT ARE THE THINGS, ACTIVITIES, OR PEOPLE THAT MAKE YOU UNHAPPY, UPSET, UNCOMFORTABLE, SAD, MAD, AND EVEN CRY?

IF THIS QUESTION APPLIES TO YOU, EXPLAIN HOW.

DO I LIKE WHO I AM?

Some people appreciate or even love who they are. They are very comfortable with who they are; what they represent; how they see themselves, and how others see them. Some people are comfortable with their perfections, as well as their imperfections. Some recognize areas where they could use personal improvement- without viewing those needs as weaknesses.

IF YOU LIKE WHO YOU ARE, WHY? IF NOT, WHY NOT?

WHAT ARE THE THINGS I LIKE ABOUT ME?

It is possible to like things about yourself without feeling or appearing vain, self-centered, or with a complex?

Some people feel that self-admiration, self-appreciation, and affirmation are helpful toward building and establishing confidence, and character.

IF THERE ARE SOME THINGS YOU LIKE ABOUT YOURSELF, WHAT ARE THEY, AND WHY?

WHAT ARE THE THINGS ABOUT ME I WISH WERE DIFFERENT?

Some people set high standards for themselves, and are never satisfied with who they are, and where they land. This high-standard setting could lead to a quest to overachieve, or to a state of discontent.

Some people are constantly trying to measure up to standards set by others. If successful, this quest could lead to a sense of achievement, or if not successful, one could feel a sense of failure.

IF YOU RECOGNIZE SOME THINGS THAT YOU WISH WERE DIFFERENT, WHAT ARE THOSE THINGS?

WHAT IS SELF-ESTEEM?

Synonyms or near-synonyms of self-esteem include: self-worth, self-regard, self-respect, and self-integrity." According to The American Heritage Dictionary of the English Language, "self-love" is "the instinct or desire to promote one's well-being."

In simple language, self-esteem is what or how people see and feel about themselves. In fact, self- esteem can also be expressed through a person's behavior or actions.

HOW DO YOU SEE OR FEEL ABOUT YOURSELF?

ARE THERE DIFFERENT KINDS OF SELF-ESTEEM?

HIGH SELF-ESTEEM

High self-esteem represents positive thinking and actions- in the moment. Sometimes a person's behavior will show obvious signs of positive self-esteem. For instance, Mr. Jones' voice is elevated with energy; he speaks in positive, and optimistic terms. He walks with confidence, and wears a genuine smile.

CAN YOU THINK OF OTHER WAYS TO RECOGNIZE A PERSON WITH HIGH SELF-ESTEEM?

PLEASE LIST THEM.

LOW SELF-ESTEEM

Converse to high self-esteem, low self-esteem can represent negative thinking and actions, in the moment. Sometimes a person's behavior will show obvious signs of negative self-esteem. For instance, Mrs. Jones' voice is elevated with energy; she speaks in negative, and pessimistic terms. She walks in a way that makes her appear to be nervous, and doubts herself. And on her face, she shows anger, and despair.

CAN YOU THINK OF OTHER WAYS TO RECOGNIZE A PERSON WITH LOW SELF-ESTEEM/
PLEASE LIST THEM.

HOW TO RECOGNIZE SELF-ESTEEM?

Self-esteem is essentially a feeling, and a behavior possessed and expressed by a subject person, and witnessed by observers. When a behavior of another is observed, usually the observed behavior is met with a measure of judgement- that the behavior is good behavior, or bad behavior, positive or negative behavior, and often referred to as high self-esteem versus low self-esteem.

This combination of observed behavior and judgement invites the idea to label the person who is being observed. This observation and judgement, on its face, may prove to be incorrect –in terms of labeling the subject as having high self-esteem, or low self-esteem. Often, when the labeling is placed, the status of "Temporary or in the moment," may not have been considered. It is perhaps reasonable to imagine that someone can demonstrate the qualities of high self-esteem and low self esteem in the same day, based on the situation or conditions at the time.

If diagnosis is being proposed, in some cases, the diagnosis could be wrong. In fact, a misdiagnosis may be the result of bias from the observer who may not be informed, or educated about other cultural customs or traditions.

For example, Thomas is being observed as he appears to cry easily, lately. For the past three weeks at work, he works in isolation, and sits in the corner, and eats alone in the workplace cafeteria. He obviously shows sadness.

The observer takes notice, and concludes that Thomas shows low energy, appears to exhibit anti-social behavior, and shows low confidence, and is therefore experiencing low self-esteem.

In this case, the observer's observation and labeling, and subsequent diagnosis of Thomas as a person with low self-esteem is inaccurate, because Thomas is from a culture which has a custom that requires its people to behave as Thomas did- to mourn, grieve, and heal from the loss of a family member. So, in this case, Thomas doesn't have low self-esteem. In fact, he has high self-esteem, as he feels self- respect, and self-value for his loyalty, and observance to his cultural customs.

So, the question becomes, how does Thomas feel about what Thomas is doing? In other words, the answer to the question about Thomas' self-esteem should not be left up to the observer. Again, it's about what Thomas is experiencing. However, it is possible that the observer could be spot on, and Thomas does have low self-esteem-based on his behavior. Thomas may propose, or perhaps admit he has low self-esteem.

IS SELF-ESTEEM OBJECTIVE OR SUBJECTIVE?

SELF-ESTEEM CAN BE BOTH OBJECTIVE AND SUBJECTIVE AT THE SAME TIME.

Self-esteem as objective can perhaps be understood by what is somewhat factual and obvious to the eyes. For example, Professor John shows confidence and courage in his knowledge base, and speaking tone when he delivers his lecture in front of large crowds. The fact that Professor John shows confidence, it may be easy to objectively suggest that he has high self-esteem.

Conversely, Self-esteem as subjective can perhaps be understood by something less obvious, but more based on inner thoughts, and judgement. For example, Dean Adler thinks Professor John is a good lecturer with high self-esteem because Professor John seems to show confidence sharing his lectures.

If you think about it, both objective and subjective self-esteem in application can be met by a thin line. For instance, if objective self-esteem is based upon something factually obvious, then the assumption is that the effort or action that is factually obvious, is genuine. However, if the effort or action is not genuine, or simply fake, then is the objective self-esteem real? For instance, if Linda's appearance to be positive with high self-esteem is in fact an act or disguise, then the objective labeling or judgement is misguided.

Similarly, if Wanda, who is genuinely a positive person with high self-esteem, decides for the purpose of gaining sympathy or pity, behaves in a negative manner by pretending to be negative with low energy, self-condemnation, and even verbalizing suicidal thoughts... and is eventually successful at achieving the pity from others who believed their own thoughts about Wanda, then the labeling or judgement is misguided, in this scenario.

THIN LINE BETWEEN HIGH SELF-ESTEEM AND ARROGANCE.

LOW SELF-ESTEEM REPRESENTS NEGATIVE CONNOTATIONS SUCH AS LOW ENERGY, DOUBT, FEAR, LACK OF AMBITION, OR LACK OF CONFIDENCE, TO NAME A FEW.

We live a world where positive energy, productivity, progress, and achievement are cherished aims and goals, and those who demonstrate these qualities are often recognized, and even praised. Conversely, any hint of negativity is frowned upon. People tend to aspire towards the sphere of positivity. In addition to the obvious positive attitudes and actions, some people intentionally offer and self- promote their positive qualities that could rather easily suggest high self-esteem. Sometimes the mention, reminding, self-promotion is so intense, there can be an appearance of boasting, flaunting, pride, and even arrogance. Arrogance creates a thin line to high self-esteem. Arrogance then takes on a negative context. Some people, especially those who are shy, or self-conscious, recognize this, and in some way show humility- to play down a little showing of high self-esteem, to avoid the negative labeling of arrogance.

WHAT DOES HIGH SELF-ESTEEM LOOK LIKE?

High self-esteem can be audibly evidenced through someone's words used to express messages of self-identity, confidence, self-worth and other words of positive energy. Additionally, someone's positive energy-based behavior can be visible signs of what high self-esteem looks like.

WHAT DOES LOW SELF-ESTEEM LOOK LIKE?

Converse to high self-esteem, low self-esteem can be audibly evidenced through someone's words used to express negative messages of self-identity, lack of confidence, little self-worth and other words of negative energy. Additionally, someone's negative energy-based behavior can be visible signs of what low self-esteem looks like.

ARE THE SIGNS OF SELF-ESTEEM GENUINE/REAL OR FAKE?

When a person behaves in a particular way, is the behavior genuine, or is it exaggerated, such that an observer's judgement could be wrong? Similarly, when a person's behavior is observed, is the judgement an exaggeration such that the observer is wrong?

ARE THE SIGNS OF SELF-ESTEEM USED AS MANIPULATORS?

Is it possible for someone-with their motives, to use what appears to be signs of self-esteem, high or low, to manipulate a situation? Perhaps the answer could be yes. For instance, Alex absolutely hates his job as a fashion model. His job as a fashion model requires him to project an image of self- confidence, and courage, and constant smiling…and he projects them well. However, his reality is that he does not truly believe in himself, and in real time, a pessimist, but yet, he plays the role of appearing confident to his benefit – to thrive in the fashion world. So, in this case, he manipulates the situation.

Conversely, Alex, is naturally positive, but wants to transition from his current profession as a fashion model, so he manipulates the situation, and pretends to despise this job- for the purpose of being reassigned to a different job function.

Are the signs of self-esteem results of manipulations?

Oftentimes, people are controlled by others or situations, such that their thoughts and behaviors are results of manipulations, and not self- representative. In other words, some people may profess certain affirmations such as positive declarations that they are positive, and speak confidently about themselves and life. Additionally, they may portray a persona of high energy, and ambition. These portrayals may be the result of manipulation, so they may be simply doing what they are told, or what is expected from them. For instance, someone may be a corporate manager, who is expected to represent the spirit of a leader with confidence, and ambition. However, this manager is not fully qualified to be in that position, so she is often self-doubting her abilities; she lacks the self-confidence that might otherwise suggest that she has high self-esteem, when in fact, she has low self-esteem. The pressure and stress from the job causes loneliness, and depression. In this case, self-esteem is a result of situational manipulation.

WHERE DOES SELF-ESTEEM COME FROM?

IS SELF-ESTEEM TEMPORARY, PERMANENT, SHORT TERM, LONG TERM?

Self-esteem is personal, and it is connected to personal thoughts, feelings, emotions, and behaviors. Generally speaking, when dealing with emotions or feelings, the idea that emotions or feelings can be permanent, is not reasonable, nor practical, because they are always subject to change, and they do. Sure, self-esteem can be temporary, short- term, and even long-term.

DR. JAMES E. BRUCE, SR.

IS SELF-ESTEEM A PERCEPTION?

Perhaps self-esteem can be based on a perception, somewhat consistent with subjectivity from an observer who may observe and reserve or pass judgement about the behavior of another. The judgement could be positive or negative. It could be based in facts or myths- based on how the observer perceives the behavior.

Self –esteem can be a perception from the subject – based on how the subject perceives his or her behavior, as positive or negative. The self- perception could be based on the truth or myths. Additionally, a perception of self-esteem can be inspired or influenced by manipulation, and the manipulation can influence an inaccurate reading on the perceived self-esteem of a subject.

IS SELF-ESTEEM AN ASSUMED OR PRESUMED HUMAN QUALITY?

Four natural and obvious features of being human include the ability to think, assess, judge, and act. With all things being equal, we think about the things we see, hear, feel, even taste and smell. We make assessments and judgements about things, other people, and even ourselves. In most cases we pass judgement regarding the things we encounter.

In this process, oftentimes the thoughts, assessments, judgements, and acts are made in relationship to ourselves. The test results manifest into the questions, what do I think? How do I feel, and what will I do?

We may be able to conclude that self-esteem is an assumed or presumed human quality since self-esteem involves one's feeling of how one feels about oneself. In this context, the term feeling can be interchanged with the words see, view, or value, as in how does one see, view, or value oneself. This approach is essentially the core meaning of self-esteem.

CAN SELF-ESTEEM BE DIAGNOSED OR MISDIAGNOSED?

If diagnosis or misdiagnosis of self-esteem is a potential outcome from a human being about another human being, the answer is yes.

Usually, the term diagnose is associated with a social or medical professional, or human behavior specialist. A diagnosis is often a more formal determination of an observation based on a certain pattern of behaviors. It is quite possible for an observation of a person's behavior to be inaccurately described.

The term diagnose is contrasted to the term judgement. Judgement is perhaps more subjective, and a diagnosis seems more objective.

Self-esteem can be diagnosed by a subject person. A person can self-diagnose self-esteem, especially if they understand and know what it is. Similarly, a person can self- misdiagnose self-esteem, if they are conflicted with their feelings, and struggle with facing and accepting reality.

IS SELF-ESTEEM AN ASSET OR LIABILITY?

The answer to this question will perhaps depend- if the self-esteem is viewed by the subject or the observer as positive or negative. Obviously, if it is considered positive, it will be embraced as an asset. Conversely, if self-esteem is viewed as negative, it will be considered a liability. This question can be objective or subjective. If human bias, or judgements are allowed, then there is a chance for an incorrect determination that may suggest the opposite of what is.

For instance, Michael has high self-esteem, he is confident, full of positive energy, and believes in himself. He is subjective, and feels strongly about his position, and therefore sees his self-esteem as an asset. Cynthia, however, objectively observes Michael's behavior and is judgmental, and sees him as arrogant, and therefore determines that Michael's self-esteem is negative, and as such, a liability. What's more, Michael's positive self-esteem may have an impact upon Cynthia's inferiority complex. She may therefore be intimidated by Michael's positive energy.

WHO DOES SELF-ESTEEM AFFECT?

Because self-esteem is mainly about the subject person, - self; it initially affects the subject person, knowingly or unknowingly. Sometimes, some people may not realize they have tendencies, or behaviors which display low self-esteem. They regularly put themselves down. They can

DR. JAMES E. BRUCE, SR.

superficially show modesty, grace or humility towards someone else; this may be done as a way to show deference to someone else. Some people may openly show a lack of self- confidence, and they regularly doubt themselves. One's self-esteem has a natural ability, at minimum, to indirectly impact others, especially if the subject person has the power and influence over others. Many people are impressed, inspired, influenced, encouraged, motived, or diminished by the thoughts and behaviors of others.

HOW TO PREVENT OR AVOID LOW SELF-ESTEEM?

The first step towards preventing or avoiding low self-esteem is to understand what it is. And make sure what is proposed, labeled, referenced, described, and determined to be low self-esteem is in fact low self-esteem, preferably from the perspective of the subject person, and not from an observer.

The subject person is perhaps the best person to truly know what low-self- esteem is- based on their feelings, and especially if they understand their behavior. The observer may react from a subjective, or biased position to the obvious behavior of the subject person.

Again, the classification of low self-esteem can perhaps be best qualified by the subject person. If low self-esteem is associated with negative feelings or behaviors, then the subject person is the one to indicate if they feel positive or negative, and if their behavior is rightly labeled low self-esteem, then the subject person is the one to decide if they understand what it is, and if they are okay with it, or if they want to change to feel differently.

HOW TO MANAGE SELF-ESTEEM?

Self-esteem exists in different forms, in other words, high self-esteem, low self-esteem, and some will even say normal self-esteem. The question how to manage self-esteem assumes that self-esteem is manageable. And the subsequent question is what does managed self-esteem look like? The next query is who has the power or ability to manage self-esteem? The assumption is that the subject person has the power to manage one's self-esteem.

It has also been proposed that the self-esteem of one can be influenced and manipulated by someone else. If that is true, then the question becomes, is manipulation a form of management?

If one has the power and the ability to control one's feelings, and behavior, and if feelings and behavior are related to one's self-esteem, then the subject person may be able to self-manage her behavior in order to continue to feel or refrain from feeling a certain way that impacts how one sees or feels about self.

Additionally, if someone else has power and influence over a subject person's behavior, thoughts and feelings, through manipulation, or even intimidation, then, in essence, the subject person's self-esteem can be managed by another.

HOW TO MAINTAIN SELF-ESTEEM?

The question, how to maintain self-esteem invariably assumes that self-esteem is maintainable, and there is a subtle desire that self-esteem be maintained.

Of course, there is a need to know and understand what self-esteem is, and what kind of self-esteem are we talking about? Are we talking about low self-esteem, or high self-esteem? Certainly, there is a question, however, and possibly rhetorical. Are there benefits for anyone to maintain low self-esteem? This is perhaps a fair question since it is conceivable that someone may find a benefit in maintaining low self-esteem.

And what does maintaining self-esteem look like? And if self-esteem can be maintained, for how long? Who has the power to maintain self-esteem?

HIGH SELF-ESTEEM VS SELF-CONFIDENCE, OVER- CONFIDENCE, PRIDE, AMBITION, ARROGANCE, POMPOUS, VANITY, NARCISSISM, OR EGOTISM.

Self-esteem is generally understood to be the what and how people view and feel about themselves. That is, if they see themselves with value. In addition to their feelings and judgement of themselves, are their actions and behavior. Are they motivated, enthusiastic, and full of energy?

DR. JAMES E. BRUCE, SR.

There are attempts to identify and discover some people with high self-esteem, especially for some people who can easily recognize high self- esteem. Other people who may not quite understand high self-esteem may assume and label a person with high self-esteem as proud, arrogant, pompous, vain, a narcissist, or an egotist. So, there may be a thin line of distinction that could inappropriately label or characterize someone who may naturally be a positive, and confident person. Positive self-esteem is associated with positive words, terms, and behaviors.

WHAT AFFECTS SELF-ESTEEM?

What affects self-esteem as a question gets a simple answer with many parts as examples. The simple answer is, anything that has the ability to the impact one's own, or someone else's feelings, emotions, thoughts and behavior. For instance, food, events, situations, activities, and even people can inspire or improve, diminish or destroy one's self-esteem. A given status of self-esteem can be reinforced or reconfigured.

HOW TO REVERSE LOW SELF-ESTEEM?

The question, how to reverse low self-esteem presumes that low self-esteem is reversable, and it is a status to be aimed for. Because self-esteem derives through thoughts, feelings, emotions, and behavior, behavior becomes a manifestation of one's thoughts, feelings, and emotions, of which all can be modified to produce different results of self-esteem at various levels, ranging from low to high, and back to low. If low self-esteem is reversable, then who has the power to reverse it?

THE TRANSFORMATION OVERVIEW

REBUILDING YOUR TEMPLE WITH SELF-ESTEEM from the Inside Out should result in a transformation of ones' social, emotional, psychological and spiritual being.

The operative word is Self-Esteem. What is self-esteem? For the functional definition and understanding for this book; self-esteem concerns YOU, and everything that comprises you. In other words, you consist of the food you eat, the clothes you wear; the home you live in; the books you read; the movies you view; the music you listen to; the friendships you keep etc. The ultimate and obvious common and reasonable goal is to love life, and live life to the fullest. But then again, what is common and what is reasonable? What is meant by: to "love and to live life to the fullest?" Because self –esteem is so deeply impacted by social or cultural experiences, the matter of self –esteem is relative. In other words, one culture might frown upon another culture for the way its people are treated badly. For the persons who receive the bad treatment, based on the way they react or fail to act, observers might suggest that those subject persons have no respect for themselves. On-lookers might say, "Those persons have low self-esteem; they lack courage or confidence." to effect a change.

Defining self-esteem could sometimes be a challenge because the accepted definitions are not absolute. Theoretically, self-esteem relates to a feeling, mood or disposition, stimulated as a response to something. And self-esteem manifests in a behavior. Although a person's behavior is not always self- directed or controlled.

Generally speaking, a person's behavior can always be explained or justified, not necessarily accepted or appreciated. For instance, a prostitute who uses his or body for sex to make money might be viewed and judged to have low self-esteem, or no self- respect. That statement alone could be inaccurate. In fact, that person could be very much respectful of self, but might be desperate for money, at the time, and his or her body might be the only thing they have at the time to bargain with. Again, one's behavior could raise questions about self-esteem.

The operative word here is Rebuilding. To rebuild implies that something or someone has been diminished; has become inferior; lost its power; strength; flavor; honor; appreciation; foundation or value. Further, to rebuild implies that something or someone is not the same, or needs to redefine its function or purpose to accommodate something or someone that has changed. Just image, if your home gets struck by a hurricane or tornado, and the windows get shattered, part of the roof gets lifted, and several of the cornerstones in the foundation get shifted… a decision has to be made. But before a rational decision is made, a damage assessment must be conducted. The bottom-line challenge will be to determine if the damages to the house are severe enough to declare a total loss or not. If there is not a total loss, then there is likely some significant portion of the house that could be rebuilt by using the same or better-quality parts. The rebuild option is an alternative to the other options to repair, restore or replace.

To repair or restore is to use the same parts, and return the quality or design to where it used to be. And replace as an option, is to provide a same, similar, or new and different design that will produce the same or better performance. In essence, these are the available options to the human experience, especially if there is a need to rebuild one's temple with self-esteem from the inside out.

The end result of this kind of thinking –whether we are talking about objects or humans, is that we should be looking for original or better functioning.

Chapter one, **_Discovering the Imbalance,_** involves a scenario about the literal rebuilding of a portion of a falling down house. Implementing the rebuilding process by applying the repair, restore or replace approach allows for a methodical design change.

Chapter two, Who is in Mr. Washington's House, involves a scenario that virtually mirrors the scenario in chapter one. But the goal in chapter two is to: Rebuild the Human Temple with Self-Esteem from the Inside Out. To arrive at this goal, the response is sought for the: who, what, when, where, why and how self-esteem is central to one's being. In chapter two, our subject person Tonia journeys through the exercise and is shown how to rebuild her temple with self-esteem from the inside out.

A complete transformation does not take full effect until one is no longer troubled by what others, the negative ones, feel, say, or do. A true transformation is not realized until one is able to actively demonstrate self-respect and self-confidence, as well as through other signs such as love expressed for self and others. Self-respect can be established by setting standards and expectations. The expectations include perhaps an endless list of acceptable or unacceptable actions or inactions; behaviors; demands; assumptions; realities; judgments; treatments; temptations; courtesies; favors; responsibilities; challenges- physical; mental; emotional; psychological; spiritual; social; sexual; economical and more. Again, the list is virtually endless.

Chapter Two

DISCOVERING THE IMBALANCE

JUST IMAGINE YOU ARE AT home and looking out of your window at your neighbor, Mr. Washington's house across the street. You notice that his house appears to be leaning to one side. So, you stare a little harder to make sure that your eyes are not playing tricks on you. You might even slide your peripheral and visually inspect the houses on either side of this house that appears to be leaning. The houses on either side seems to be flawless. At that point you determine that yes, your neighbor, Mr. Washington's house; the one in the middle is in fact leaning. A puzzling question quickly runs through your mind: what is going on? Of course, you know that something is not quite right. To immediately satisfy your curiosity, and stroke the wits of your ego genius, you conclude that something is wrong with the foundation or the integrity of that house. You know for sure that there is an imbalance.

Since you are still trying to determine the nature of the imbalance that you have discovered, you might even speculate that perhaps the house is intact, but maybe the foundation as in the earth that supports the placement of the house is not solid. So, you might feel the urge to notify Mr. Washington about what you see from your window.

As a courtesy, you make it a point to visit your neighbor, Mr. Washington to let him know what you see. Upon alerting him, immediately he asks: are you sure? You then confirm by replying: yes, I'm sure. You proceed to tell him about your observation and the test that you applied to reach your prognosis about his house being in a state of imbalance. Mr. Washington reacts almost in denial. He insists on going to your side of the street, to stand in front of your house, in an attempt to see what you can see.

The visit results in his first- hand observation, and later inspection, and determination that the turf that supports the house structure was not the cause for the apparent leaning house. But in fact, the problem has to be on the inside of his house.

Mr. Washington determines right then that something must be done to correct the problem with his leaning house. He knows that if the problem does not get addressed appropriately, and timely, that eventually his house will collapse. He hires a construction engineer. Mr. Geer, a seasoned and prominent construction engineer knows what to look for in response to his observation of leaning walls in Mr. Washington's house. With a primary focus on the quality of the component parts of the subject matter, Mr. Geer first inspects the outside grounds for land erosion, or depletion or weaknesses in the soil. What he finds only confirms what Mr. Washington has already concluded based on Mr. Washington's land inspection. So, Mr. Geer, as does Mr. Washington, resolves that the problem is on the inside of the house.

Once on the inside of the house, Mr. Geer checks the basement's foundation for breaks, cracks or leaks. He notices a gaping crack in one of the side cement walls. He also sees that several wood column beams are cracked towards the lower part, about eight inches from the concrete floor. He looks up at the basement's ceiling and observes that the ceiling cross- beams on the side of the house is cracked where the cement wall is, It shows an obvious slope. That alone, provides some insight and understanding for why the wall upstairs was leaning. He begins to produce a preliminary report for Mr. Washington, which will be followed by recommendations towards rebuilding, restoring or replacing the foundation, the imperfect vertical and cross ceiling- beams in the basement, and the interior and exterior of the wall upstairs.

A few days later, Mr. Washington receives Mr. Geer's construction engineer's report and recommendation. The report recommends that Mr. Washington hires a contractor/carpenter to remove the sheetrock from the leaning wall in order to determine the quality of the interior wood studs. The contractor/carpenter will be required to rebuild, restore or replace the studs, along with all the damaged basement structure previously determined by Mr. Geer.

Fortunately, Mr. Washington knows a qualified contractor/carpenter who can perform the services prescribed by the construction engineer, Mr. Geer. Miss Brooks has more than twenty years of master contractor/carpenter expertise. She gladly accepts the job. On the agreed date, she brings in her construction crew of three. Within minutes, they remove the sheetrock from the leaning wall, thus exposing all the wood studs. She observes that of the twenty wood studs, six are cracked from the bottom to about three feet from the floor. Four studs are rotted out from the moisture that passes from the interior water pipes, and three studs located nearest the window opening were attacked by termites. The remaining seven wood studs are near perfect from when they were first installed twenty-five years ago.

Miss Brook's training and expertise guides her through the appropriate stages to remedy the leaning wall and sloping floor. She knows that the proper approach is be to rebuild, restore or replace. She knows already that when the appropriate measures are taken, the wall, floor/ceiling and foundation will be like new. The master carpenter, Miss Brooks, begins assessing the quality of the inside wall studs. She instructs her apprentice carpenters to rebuild three of the cracked studs. The other three cracked studs are so badly ruined that they have to be replaced. All four of the rotted-out studs—caused by moisture require replacement. And the three studs that were attacked by termites are restorable.

After three days of precision work, the upstairs wall, the floor/ceiling and the gaping crack in one of the basement's cement walls looks brand new. Mr. Washington is pleased with the quality of the work that went into rebuilding, restoring and replacing the damage that existed on the inside of his house. Mr. Washington couldn't seem to thank you enough for acknowledging his problem, and taking the first step towards affecting a positive outcome. At the end of Mr. Washington's homeowner's experience, he realizes that the value of his property was at minimum returned or at best enhanced.

Chapter Three

WHO IS IN MR. WASHINGTON'S HOUSE?

THE SCENARIO IN CHAPTER TWO offered a simplistic example of the gist of this book. The story involved the rebuilding of parts of a natural house that suffered a diminished quality and value. To recall the story, there was a process in play. The first act began the process of proactive engagement. The act started with your observation, -the leaning house, followed by assessment, investigation, determination, further observation, notification, inquiry, and recommendation. These acts and more resulted in the rebuilding, replacement and restoration of quality and value to Mr. Washington's house.

Mr. Washington's physical house was used as a metaphoric symbol to demonstrate the human experience as concerning one's self-esteem. One's self-esteem relates to self-respect and self-confidence, and a host of other human qualities that help determine or affect the social, spiritual, emotional, psychological standing in our complex society. As stated in the sub-title, this book is a practical how to guide to rebuilding and restoring one's self-esteem (value) when it has suffered a decline. Further, this book is designed to provide turn-around solutions to the challenges that affect self-esteem, by addressing the: who, what, when, where, why and how self-esteem is central to ones' being.

This chapter presents a scenario that involves rebuilding the human temple with self-esteem. So, the question: who is in Mr. Washington's house? This begs the deeper question of what is the quality of the component parts that make up one's self-esteem.

Earlier we established that self-respect and self-confidence are only two of many terms that pertain to self-esteem. The goal is to seek and apply proven practices and strategies that will ultimately improve the quality of life. Life improvement can be achieved when one is taught or encouraged to love, appreciate, and respect oneself. Another major goal is to help people to improve the level of self-confidence.

 To arrive at the answers for credible solutions, in this chapter we will analyze the quality of the questions: Perhaps the question: what? as in what is the quality… will provide that most informative data.

Ok, just imagine you observe a colleague or an associate at work; a family member or friend who regularly walks with her head down; always talks in negative terms; constantly lacks confidence in her abilities, and demonstrates a poor representation of love, appreciation and respect for herself and others. This same person walks with bad posture; takes little pride in her appearance; eating healthy foods is not a priority; full of doubt; complains about being lonely or bored, and expresses fear, to name a few examples.

If you know someone like the person just described, you might be like Mr. Washington's concerned neighbor. You might first observe what you are witnessing. And then you might focus a bit to make sure you understand your observation. You will want to confirm what you see and hear. Like Mr. Geer, the engineer, you will be focused on the quality of the component parts of the concern. Like Mr. Washington, you will have concluded as obvious that something is not right. In other words, something about your colleague or associate at work; a family member or friend represents a diminished quality and value. And that there is some aspect of their life that needs to be repaired, restored or replaced.

To begin to assess the process towards understanding what is going on, you will apply the phases as was used in chapter two, in the scenario involving Mr. Washington's leaning house. You will then inquire and note the measurable quality of virtually every aspect of the component parts of what comprises the subject person.

Consider that every part of the individual human experience has the potential to impact the individual's self-esteem. So, the test is more about the quality than quantity. Some examples of component parts of the individual human experience include the food we eat; the clothes we wear; the neighborhood we live in; the books we read; the movies we view; the friends we have; the car we drive; the careers we pursue, etc.

Again, it's not the quantity or how many movies one watches; it's the quality. So, in the end, the question is: what or how did the movie impact the quality of one"s life? Similarly, the question is not so much the amount of water one drinks, but the quality of the water. Additionally, having twenty friends has little value if the twenty friends are not true, decent, helpful and reliable as friends. Lastly, the fact that John has four paying jobs has less value if he hates all four jobs when compared to Robert who has only one job that he enjoys.

To test the scenario using the: who, what, when, where, why and how self-esteem is central to one's being? Let's take Tonia for instance; she fits the earlier description. We want to look for a moment to understand why Tonia is expressing boredom with the fact that she has seven friends. Ok, we look at who are those friends? What do they represent? What do they do for Tonia? If they claim to be Tonia's friends, when do they prove themselves to be friends or friendly? Where are they when Tonia really needs them? Why do they want to be Tonia's friends? And how do they prove to be Tonia's friends? And how do they add to the quality of life for Tonia?

Let's look at that for a moment. Is Tonia more focused on the number or quality of her friends? What do they expect from the friendship? To be objective in this analysis, we must seek to understand the quality that Tonia brings to the friendship. What does Tonia bring to and expect from the friendship?

It seems that since Tonia has seven mutual friends, she should never be bored or feeling lonely. When pressed with questions, it turns out that the public behaviors of five of her friends have taken a turn for the worse. These five friends are obnoxious, loud, rude and embarrassing while in public. There are however other qualities that Tonia enjoys. At the same time, Tonia prefers to not visit their homes. When in public, Tonia shuts down, and doesn't say much. When at the restaurant or movies, she tends to sit to the side so as to not be noticed. She feels that public observers are judging her and labeling her as out of control along with her friends. Tonia's other two friends are not mutual friends to the five loud friends. In fact, they are independent of the other. These two friends are decent, but Tonia can never seem to get with their hectic schedules. So that explains why Tonia might be bored and lonely.

Now, Tonia could attempt to reverse the situation. She could approach the five rude friends and apply, as did Miss Brooks, the test to: rebuild, restore or replace. Tonia could meet with them individually or as a group and express to them a preferred behavior. She could suggest to them ways that their friendshp could be rebuilt with new and exciting ideas and activities. She could critically tell them what behaviors need to change-in an effort to restore what they originally had as friends. As a third or harder approach, Tonia could give them an ultimatum, and let them know individually or collectively that they must change their rude and obnoxious behaviors or she will have to replace them with other friends that will not impact negatively on their friendship relationship.

Remember that self-esteem has to do with self-respect and self-confidence. The question concerning Tonia, how self-esteem is central to one's being?

The question becomes: how dependent on her friends is she in order for her to be happy, and demonstrate her happiness in her actions and her words. Does she have the love, self- respect, appreciation and self-confidence for herself to be happy with herself? Okay, the discussion of the topic of friends for Tonia is not exhausted.

The next subject area for mention and analysis for Tonia could be the quality of food that she eats. Applying the: who, what, when, where, why and how self-esteem is central to one's being? The first question is who, as in who buys and prepares Tonia's food? The: who question for quality is important because knowing who Tonia is and what she requires is critical and central to Tonia's being. The what question relates to what is in the food? In other words, because food content creates a direct impact on the way people feel, see and appreciate themselves; knowing what she requires is important. If food composition and servings pose a weight or nutrition management issue, then knowing food quality or what is in Tonia's food is central to her being.

The when question asks about when Tonia eats and the best times for her to eat. For instance, Tonia might require a heavy breakfast in the morning, otherwise she might become irritated and moody in the morning. An empty stomach or an imbalanced meal might translate into anxiety or lack of confidence for Tonia. Where Tonia eats might have a significant impact on what and when she eats. For example, Tonia's work schedule might dictate that she eats only available fast food while on the road. Eating fast food is certainly a quality issue; it might have a negative effect on Tonia's daily productivity. Why, is the question for Tonia. She has to answer why she eats the quality food that she eats? The reason might be affordability, availability, or the ability to consume. The last question here is how does she eat? Again, the test question is not how much; the question is the quality. Does Tonia take her time and digest her food? Does she feel good about the quality of food she eats?

Applying the repair, restore and replace model, towards rebuilding Tonia's temple with self-esteem from the inside out, Tonia could focus on the food quality. If the content is not conducive towards healthy eating, then Tonia could look to rebuild the quality of the food she consumes. She could seek to restore the content levels of healthy eating that could help her maintain her weight much better. And finally, she could analyze the quality of the food she consumes, and the test is simple. If the food quality has no nutritional value, then what's the point…get rid of it by replacing the unhealthy food with healthy food.

By the time Tonia successfully completes the process of going through other factors to be tested, she should be able to move forward from the state of low self-esteem to a more improved status. As a result of the experience Tonia should experience a personal transformation of going from embarrassed to be empowered, or from lonely to lively.

Above were only two examples of many possible factors that can be considered for what has the power to affect one's self-esteem, particularly as relating to the task to rebuild your temple with self-esteem, from the inside out.

The following is a short list of possible factors that can impact one's self-esteem. While examining these factors, critically assess the quality rather than the quantity. For instance, the question should focus on the quality of the home, and not the room sizes, or number of homes one has. A reasonable assumption is that people derive actual benefit from the quality of what they have, or do. And the obvious goal is to have a positive experience.

* Home
* Car
* Clothing
* Education
* Family
* Money
* Books
* Movies
* Toys
* Relationships

Chapter Four

I AM THE JUDGE OF ME

S OMEONE ONCE SAID THAT WHEN you know that you know that you know that you know… imagine the rest might go like this: then convincing you otherwise is difficult to impossible. Self-esteem, according to 2002, Second Edition Webster's New World Dictionary and Thesaurus relates to self- confidence. Self –confidence borders a very thin line between arrogance, pompous, presumptuous vanity, proud, or really being sure of oneself.

Just a thought, when does the thin line gets crossed- if someone claims that they really know something, or feel extremely good about something? Why do some people seek compliment, commendation, praise, cheering on? When that happens, does that say something about the speaker? Does it suggest that the speaker has some doubt or little confidence in the abilities of the person being cheered on? Does the person who is being cheered on really need it? Is it the energy that is being sought? When that person who is being cheered, and appreciation and gratitude is being expressed in return, is that a way for the person being cheered -on to say: thanks, I really needed that? Does that verbal, non-verbal communication exchange conveys to the greeter that the receiver is really not self-confident enough to succeed in the subject area?

Conversely, if the receiver is the judge of the receiver (self), and does not look for nor accept recognition, praise, encouragement or mention; does that mean that the receiver is in fact so self-confident, and does not question his/her abilities? Or is he or she flat-out arrogant or presumptuous? And so, what if he or she is? Does that change much?

Can self-confidence be viewed as a bluff? Or, can a bluff be perceived as self-confidence? In terms of competition, in most cases, the self-confidence/bluff results in an upset for one of the competing parties. For instance, two prominent and professional boxers are interviewed before a boxing match, both will speak in powerful terms and tone, and declare to the other, that the other will be defeated. One fighter might say that the other will lose in the first round. The other fighter might say that the champion will lose the title. Now the reality is that both competing parties are qualified fighters with a track record of winning, but there will be only one winner.

So, when both fighters are interviewed before the boxing match, and both will make their claims for what the fight results will be, and what will happen to the other, the question one might ask is: did the fighters speak with conviction and confidence, over-confidence or did they bluff? And if they bluffed, did it have a psychological effect on the mind of the boxer who lost the fight?

This discussion was offered for the purposes of considering the very thin line between being self-confident and being arrogant, pompous, presumptuous, vain, proud, or really being sure of oneself. And what does that mean when the reality of defeat happens? The reality is that each person, as the judge, should know his or her own several abilities. In fact, knowledge alone is not enough. There must be effort, actions and results.

Chapter Five

SELF-ESTEEM, SELF-EXAMINATION

THIS CHAPTER PROVIDES AN OPPORTUNITY FOR THE READER TO ENGAGE IN SELF-EXAMINATION QUESTIONS, SO THE READER WILL GAIN A MORE THOROUGH UNDERSTANDING OF WHAT SELF-ESTEEM IS, AND HOW TO EFFECTIVELY MAKE ANY NECESSARY, OR APPROPRIATE CHANGES TO ENHANCE AND IMPROVE THE QUALITY OF LIFE.

Do you understand the difference between low self-esteem and high self-esteem?

Are you comfortable with the status quo?

If you could change something about your self-esteem, what would you change, when, how and why?

ASSAULT ON LOW SELF-ESTEEM
LOW SELF-ESTEEM CHECK POINT

Who is responsible for it?

When is it likely to begin?

What is low self-esteem?

What are signs of low self-esteem?

What are causes of low self-esteem?

Who determines low self-esteem?

Why do people experience low self-esteem?

How is it created, how is it defeated?

Where does it come from?

Can it go away forever?

Is low self-esteem a phase?

What does low self-esteem lead to?

ENCOURAGING OTHERS

Read the following scenario and then offer a solution using encouraging words that could help build positive self-esteem.

Debbie is a co-worker. Every day she comes into work and from the time she walks in, virtually every word that comes out her mouth is negative. The following scenario for Debbie could be typical:

Chapter Six

SELF-ESTEEM, SELF-EXAMINATION (PART 2)

ON A SCALE OF 1-10, 10 BEING MOST FAVORABLE:

How much do you value you?

I'm smart _____

I'm good looking _____

I'm happy _____

I believe I have a purpose in life _____

I believe that my voice matters _____

I care about what people think and say about me _____

What contributes to ones' state of being?

Envy/ Jealously

Sadness

Value system

Tradition

Custom Socioeconomics

Self-help

Mind, Body, Soul

The Spoken Word

Faith

Hope

Fear

Doubt

Confidence

Bad examples

Loneliness

Reality

Small stuff

Don't let material possessions define who you are as a person, they should not affect your personal value.

Consider the following suggested aspects or steps you can take to help improve your self-esteem.

Your self-esteem is a direct reflection of the thoughts and feelings you have about yourself. The thoughts you have about what you do reveal what you think and feel about yourself – your self-esteem. Positive self-esteem is an inside job. Simple steps to take to begin to improve your self-esteem.

Genuinely smile often

Make adjustments in life your

Mind your business

Tell the truth

Talk to God

Be Calm, Cool, Collected

Do at least ten things special for yourself every day. Write them down.

Learn to say "I am better than that, so I deserve better."

Explain why what you did for yourself is so special.

Express what makes you so special to deserve what you did for yourself.

How did you feel?

What were your thoughts?

When and what were the last 5 positive comments or acts you committed to someone? Was (is) your relationship to them?

IF YOU BELIEVE YOU WILL ACHIEVE YOUR LIFE'S MOUNTAINS

I KNOW I CAN, I KNOW I WILL, I KNOW I DID

Can you recall the last 5 negative made to or about you, or negative acts committed towards you?

Establish a daily ritual by saying: Today will be a fantastic day. I will receive only the good and will rebuke all the bad. I will turn every known negative into a positive. I will be mindful that others who are looking for hope and success are in need of my positive energy and smile. I will praise more and complain less. By the end of the day, I will have repeatedly commended myself for rising to the occasion to recognize the tremendous value that exists in me.

Some people are just negative and unfortunately, some can't help it, while others will have it no other way. You must be the positive change agent. So, when you see and certainly hear others, who are so negative in their words and behavior, plant a positive seed with them and say something like, speaking or behaving like that does not represent you; you are better than that. Or you deserve better than that. If you try that on someone, you will be surprised by the reaction you might get. What you are essentially saying to them is that you want to respect them, encourage them, and see them move forward.

Bad, sad or negative life experiences can be counterproductive reminders that often get in the way of one moving forward. The old saying: to forgive and forget, has serious implications on one's ability to progress in life. Try a new exercise, try to remember and live for the positive message inherent in those life experiences. By the way, remember that as long as you have life, you have an opportunity to get it right.

Perhaps the reason why so many people are so negative is because they will not see the positive side of every life experience; they tend to get stuck on the negative.

Reflection Exercise: Set aside some quiet time and have a conference with yourself.

1. Get yourself a writing tool and some writing paper
2. begin thinking back to what you consider to be some bad or negative life experience, one at a time

3. As you recall the experiences, begin writing down the negative incidents, one by one

4. Keep writing, in list format until you feel you have written all the negative incidents that you feel are worth writing down

5. Now revisit the list of negative incidents

6. Study each incident and then ask yourself, regardless of whose fault it was, did I learn anything from the experience? If so, what did I learn, and how can I turn what I learned into a positive message?

7. Next to each negative incident, write down the positive message

8. You will realize that if nothing else good came out of the experiences, you can at least say that you are alive to think and write about it

9. Challenge yourself to think about your uniqueness and how special you are; consider all that you have gone through- in the midst of defeat or near death, you are still standing. You may have fallen, but you got up.

10. Now say to yourself: I am great, and I know it; my life has meaning, so, I will show it.

AFFIRMATIONS

I love me some me, so, I will speak and show me love…

I can demonstrate my love for me if I do the following:

Say: _____
     Name

1. I am the greatest person in my life that I know

2. I am one of a kind

3. I hold the patent to my uniqueness

4. I am special

5. I am beautiful

6. I know me better than others who think they know me

7. I am talented beyond measure

8. I am a genius, so those who don't yet know me are missing out

9. I trust me

10. I know my body

11. I love my body

12. I am blessed and I know it

13. I am blessed and highly favored

14. If the world knew how special I am, they would stand in long lines to meet me

15. I am God's gift

16. I have to trust my own mind

17. I am a trillionaire, but I receive my money in installments

18. I am amazed by my intelligence

19. I am so glad to be alive

20. My life is significant in the scheme of the universe

21. I am as special as the next person

22. I was created to be a blessing to someone else

23. I am still being developed

24. I expect to be loved for who I am

25. When I fully blossom, the world better watch out

26. I'm worth it

LIST UP TO 25 OF MY POSITIVE QUALITIES THAT I AM HAPPY ABOUT:

LIST UP TO 25 OF MY NEGATIVE QUALITIES THAT I WOULD LIKE TO CHANGE

WHAT ARE YOUR KNOWN STRENGTHS?

DR. JAMES E. BRUCE, SR.

WHAT ARE YOUR KNOWN WEAKNESSES?

SET GOALS

Be discreet about private information concerning you- it might return to bite you

WHAT MIGHT TRIGGER LOW SELF-ESTEEM?

* Relationship break-up
* Loss of job
* Loss of loved one
* Suspension from school
* Major illness or accident
* Weight gain or loss
* Hair loss
* Abuse-all forms

WHAT MIGHT ENCOURAGE HIGH SELF-ESTEEM?

* A new and supportive relationship
* A new job
* A job promotion
* Awards and recognition

SELF-HELP PROCLAMATIONS TO ACHIEVE AND MAINTAIN HIGH SELF-ESTEEM

I refuse to assume responsibility for problems not created by me, nor for problems for which I am not responsible

I will think twice before I speak once

I will think before I act

I will take responsibility for all of my actions that include my thoughts, words and deeds

I will conduct myself as a professional

I will respect myself when interacting with others

I will show myself friendly

I will say: it's not what you think, it's not what you believe, it's what I know

POSITIVE SEEDS PLANTED

Words and actions are powerful instruments. Words and actions can be positive or negative, and they can have a lasting impact on a person for life. I, James Bruce, am that person on whose life positive words and actions have impacted since I was a baby-only months old.

My belated Great-Aunt, Godmother, Ernestine Williams held me in her arms, and in so many words she said to my mother that I would be very special. That was the positive seed she planted in my spirit. And when I became a little boy, my Godmother embraced me every time she saw me. She continued to honor me with the title: Master, or Prince James. These words were empowering. Throughout my adolescence years, Ernestine nurtured the seeds she planted and encouraged me with praise, and gifts for my birthdays, honor roll, and good grades achievements. Each time she hugged me, she insisted I was smart and would grow to be very successful.

The seeds that she planted in my spirit very early, blossomed within me and has established a core high self -esteem. As far back as I can remember, especially as a pre-teen, and then a teenager, I have always respected myself, and others, recognized my positive value, and displayed courage and confidence. I therefore know the value of planting positive seeds, and the lasting impact they can have from the inside- out.